# Leopards

## Victoria Blakemore

vblakemore.author@gmail.com

Copyright info/picture credits

Cover, Felix_Broenniman/Pixabay; Page 3, DaFranzos/Pixabay; Page 5, Felix_Broenniman/Pixabay; Page 7, JuniorMP/Pixabay; Page 9, Maciej Czekajewski/Adobestock; Pages 10-11, Iuliia Sokolovska/AdobeStock; Page 13, JuniorMP/Pixabay; Page 15, Free-Photos/Pixabay; Page 17, Robert1709/Pixabay; Page 19, kdsphotos/Pixabay; Page 21, Alta Oosthuizen/AdobeStock; Page 23; DKunert/Pixabay; Page 25, WiseTraveller/Pixabay; Page 27, vinzling/Pixabay; Page 29, kdsphotos/Pixabay; Page 31, PierseStevens/Pixabay; Page 33, Felix_Broenniman/ Pixabay

# Table of Contents

# What Are Leopards?

Leopards are large mammals.

They are members of the cat family.

Leopards are known for their spots. Most leopards have yellow, white, and orange fur with black spots. Some leopards are black with darker spots.

Their spots help them to blend in to the grasses and trees of their habitat.

# Size

Leopards are the smallest kind of big cat. They can be up to six feet long and three feet tall. Their tail can also be about three feet in length.

Leopards can weigh up to 165 pounds.

Male leopards are usually larger than female leopards.

# Physical Characteristics

Leopards have a long tail. It is often about the same length as their body. Their tail helps them to balance and turn quickly when running.

A leopard's ears are perked up. This allows them to have a very good sense of hearing.

A leopard's whiskers help to sense **vibrations**. They help the leopard to move in the dark without bumping into things.

7

# Habitat

Leopards are found in many different habitats. They can live in deserts, grasslands, mountains, and rainforests.

Leopards need somewhere they can hide from prey when they are hunting. This could be in the trees, behind rocks, or in tall grasses.

Leopards are found on the

continents of Africa and Asia.

Leopards are found in countries such as India, China, Uganda, Ethiopia, Sudan, and Malaysia.

# Diet

Leopards are **carnivores**. This means that they only eat meat.

Their diet is made up of gazelle, deer, and wildebeest. They have also been known to eat fish.

Leopards are **nocturnal**. They are most active at night. It is easier to sneak up on prey in the dark.

Leopards are good swimmers. They sometimes eat fish or crabs that they catch in rivers.

Leopards often hunt from trees. Their spots blend in with the leaves. This lets them pounce on their prey from above.

Leopards like to pull their food up into trees with them. This keeps it from other animals like hyenas.

# Communication

Leopards use sound and scent to communicate with each other. They can roar like other big cats. Their roar is very deep and sounds more like a bark.

Leopards mark their **territory** with their scent. It lets other leopards know to stay away.

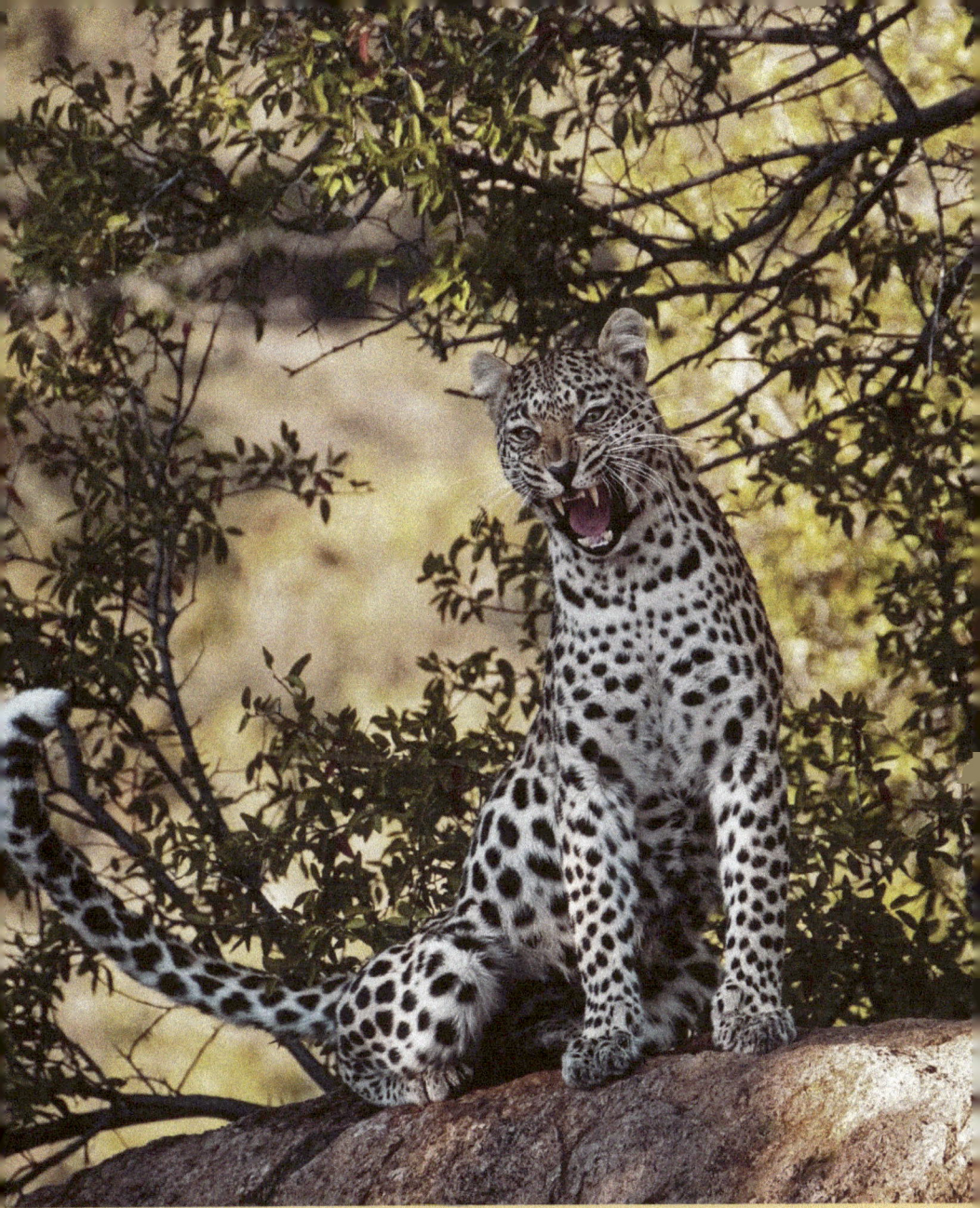

A leopard's roar can be a warning that you are in their territory.

# Movement

Leopards are able to run up to thirty-six miles per hour. Their speed helps them to catch prey.

Leopards have very strong legs. They can jump as far as twenty feet in one leap. They can jump up to ten feet high.

Leopards are one of the few

big cats that like to climb trees.

# Leopard Cubs

Leopards usually have two babies, or cubs. Their cubs are born with gray fur and very light spots.

Mothers move their cubs from place to place to keep them safe from predators.

Mothers take care of their cubs for about two years. They teach them how to hunt and survive.

# Solitary Life

Leopards are **solitary** animals. They spend most of their time alone. They do not share their territory with other leopards.

If a leopard enters another leopard's territory, they might fight.

Leopards spend most of the

day sleeping in tall trees.

# Lifespan

In the wild, leopards often live between twelve and fifteen years. In **captivity**, they can live as long as twenty-three.

They may live longer in zoos because they are safe from hunters. They also have enough food to eat.

Leopards in the wild have to hunt for their food. They don't always have enough.

# Population

Leopards have lost much of the land that used to be their habitat. Their populations are now spread out into smaller **clusters**.

In 2015, leopards were listed as **vulnerable**. They are not **endangered** yet, but their populations are **declining**.

Leopard populations are getting smaller. They could be endangered soon.

# Leopards in Trouble

Leopards were hunted for many years for their fur. This is now **illegal** in many countries. In some places, **poachers** still hunt leopards.

Leopard habitats are being destroyed for new buildings and roads.

Leopard whiskers are used in

some medicines in parts of

Africa.

# Helping Leopards

Researchers are studying leopards to learn more about them. They have special collars that they put on wild leopards. The collars help the researchers to track leopards.

They hope that learning more about where leopards are will help us to protect them.

Some groups are working to help leopards. They want to protect leopards from hunters.

They also want to help people who live near leopards to protect their livestock. If the livestock are safe from leopards, people will not kill leopards to keep them away.

# Glossary

**Captivity**: animals that are kept by humans, not in the wild

**Carnivore**: an animal that eats only meat

**Cluster**: small group

**Declining**: getting smaller

**Endangered**: at risk of becoming extinct

**Illegal**: against the law

**Nocturnal**: animals that are active at night

**Poacher:** someone who hunts animals illegally

**Solitary**: living alone

**Territory:** an area of land that an animal clams as its own

**Vulnerable**: close to becoming endangered

**Vibrations**: fast back and forth movements

# About the Author

Victoria Blakemore is a first grade

teacher in Southwest Florida with a

passion for reading.

You can visit her at

www.elementaryexplorers.com

# Also in This Series

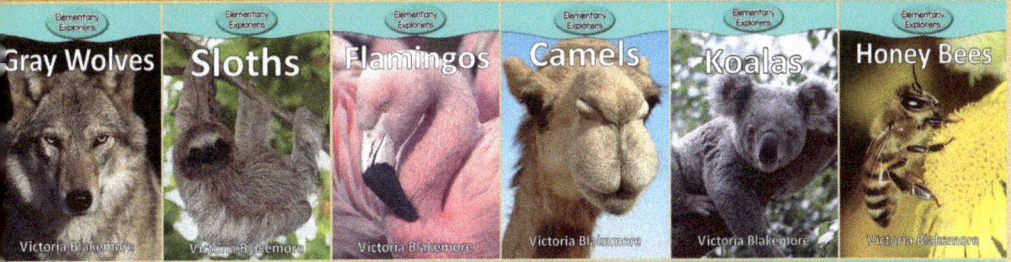

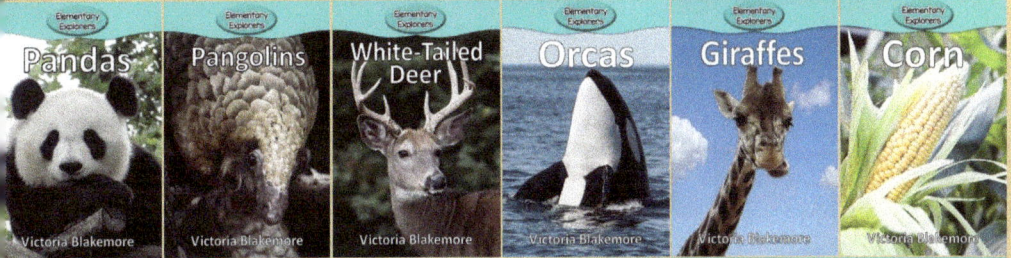

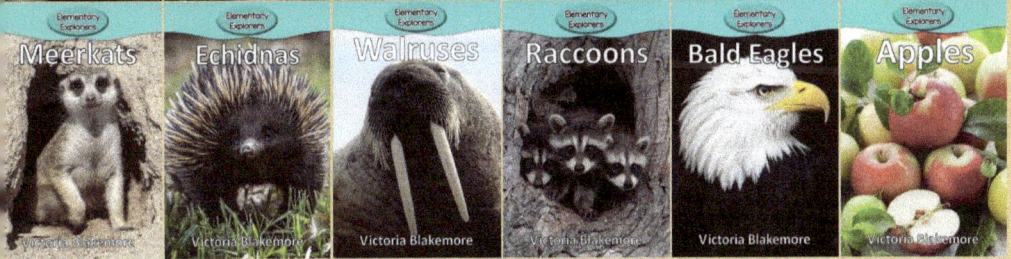

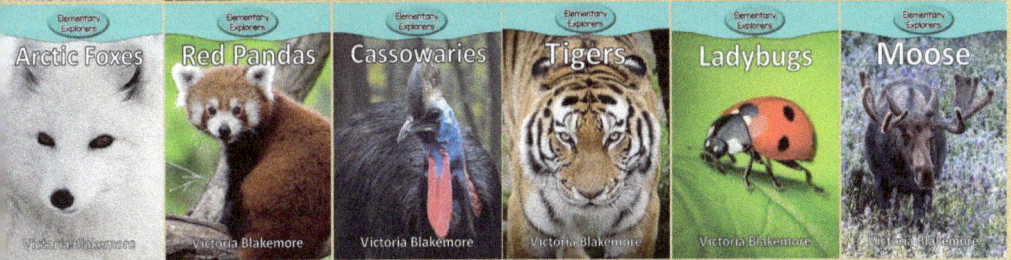

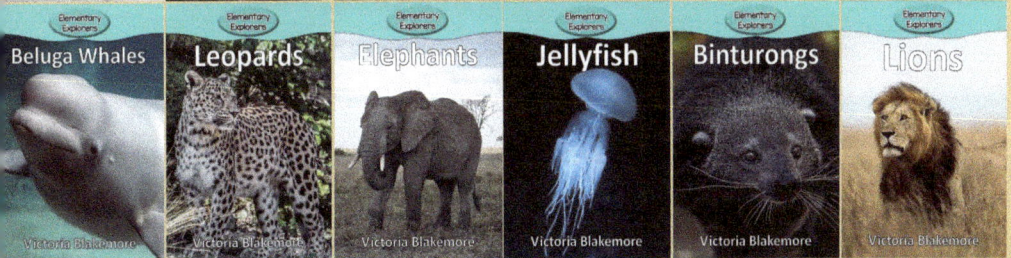

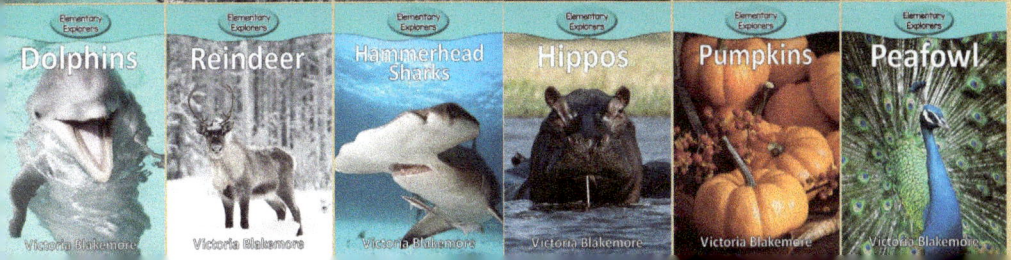

| | | | | | |
|---|---|---|---|---|---|
| Gray Wolves | Sloths | Flamingos | Camels | Koalas | Honey Bees |
| Pandas | Pangolins | White-Tailed Deer | Orcas | Giraffes | Corn |
| Meerkats | Echidnas | Walruses | Raccoons | Bald Eagles | Apples |
| Arctic Foxes | Red Pandas | Cassowaries | Tigers | Ladybugs | Moose |
| Beluga Whales | Leopards | Elephants | Jellyfish | Binturongs | Lions |
| Dolphins | Reindeer | Hammerhead Sharks | Hippos | Pumpkins | Peafowl |

Each titled: Elementary Explorers — Victoria Blakemore

# Also in This Series

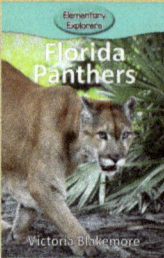

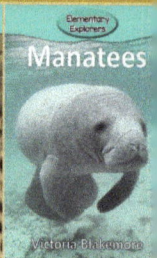

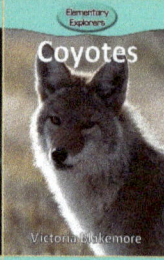

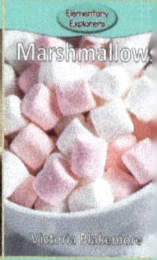

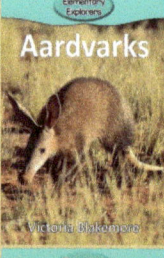

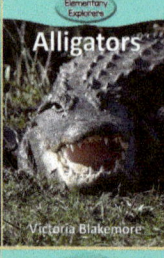

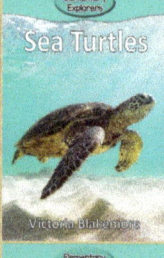

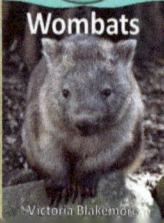

| | | | | | |
|---|---|---|---|---|---|
| Chameleons | Florida Panthers | Aye-Ayes | Black Bears | Cheetahs | Manatees |
| Gingerbread | Polar Bears | Hot Chocolate | Orangutans | Coyotes | Marshmallow |
| Strawberries | Aardvarks | Mako Sharks | Alligators | Frogs | Hedgehogs |
| Brown Bears | Bongos | Sea Turtles | Quokkas | Muskrats | Zebras |
| Red Foxes | Ring-Tailed Lemurs | Platypuses | Anteaters | Kangaroos | Rhinos |
| Jaguars | Wombats | | | | |

Elementary Explorers

Victoria Blakemore

www.ingramcontent.com/pod-product-compliance
Lightning Source LLC
Chambersburg PA
CBHW051252020426
42333CB00025B/3174